**ERICKA VALDEZ** and **JANETTE VALDEZ**

# WELCOME HOME

TO ____________________

FROM ____________________

LCCN: 2023919994

ISBN EBOOK: 9798988793991

ISBN PAPERBACK: 9798988793922

ISBN HARDCOVER: 9798988793953

www.welcomehomeadoptionbook.com

# Dedicated with love...

- **For our parents, thank you for choosing us to be your girls and for opening your hearts and family to us.**
- **For those in adoption with hopes of finding their forever family.**
- **For all the siblings out there who share a forever bond like ours.**

Once upon a time my sister was born. She was going to be my best friend for life!

I learned to look after my sister
every second because she looked
up to me. I always held her hand
so she knew I was there for her
no matter what.

I'm taller, she's smaller; I love heights she doesn't, but we both really love chocolate and catching lightning bugs at night!

She was my sister! My baby sister! We have a special story. She and I were blessed to be adopted together into a new family.

Being adopted means you were placed in a new home by your parents, placed with a family who will take care of you and love you forever.

Sis and I were grateful to our foster mom who saw our strong sister bond and knew we needed each other then and always.

Above all, we were thankful
to find there was a mom and a
dad out there in the world that
wanted us to be "their girls."

Welcome Home

Soon after, we were welcomed into our new family with a WELCOME HOME cake and hugs. Everyone made sure we knew we were home and now had a family of our own.

Our new home had a swing set, a yard, fruit trees, a garden and our own room. The best part was we now had two older brothers, a baby sister, a dog, and cats!
20

This was a day I'll never forget, the best day I ever had with my sister! I cherished every moment with her.

I knew, in our story, things had happened,  but everything was changing for the better.

From then on there wasn't a day we didn't know we were loved and cared about.

Life was amazing, always having someone to count on and share a thousand laughs with.

Our parents taught us to be kind
and say "good morning" and
"I love you" every night. Most
importantly, to be there for one
another.

We had unconditional love, we told each other everything, we dressed the same, and we even had our own nicknames. I'm her Nettie and she's my Evie.

Through it all as sisters we had ups and downs, but at the end of the day, we were inseparable and we always knew that.

I was happy with my new journey and that I had my sister by my side. We were there for one another to finish our goals and to create new ones.

Today my sister and I are all grown up and still remain best friends. We talk every day on the phone about our different tomorrow's and visit every chance we can.

We've shared many beautiful
memories throughout the years
and continue making more as
our parents are still cheering
our dreams on.

For me, my sister is the best thing that ever happened to me. I always make sure to tell my Evie I love her and hug her tight because I know we are each other's biggest fan for life.

Although Ericka and her older sister Janette are new to the adoption-advocacy world, their life experience is not. They have always wanted to share their adoption story with children of all ages, not just to those who share the experience but to all siblings out there with a bond like theirs.

Valdez explains "This book is just the beginning of what our life experience gave us to offer to the adoption advocacy. We want to be an example that a bright future is possible."

In this book the sister's share new adventures together and learn what love is through one of the biggest life changes a child could ever experience- adoption.

# YOU ARE LOVED